# *People* ⌐ ⌐ Us

Stephen Gard

Illustrated by Trish Hill

**Momentum**
People Like Us

First published in Great Britain in 1999 by

Folens Publishers
Albert House
Apex Business Centre
Boscombe Road
Dunstable
Beds LU5 4RL

© 1999 Momentum developed by Barrie Publishing Pty Limited
Suite 513, 89 High St, Kew, Vic 3101, Australia

Stephen Gard hereby asserts his moral right to be identified as the
author of this work in accordance with the Copyright, Designs and
Patents Act 1988.
© 1999 Folens Ltd. on behalf of the author.
Illustrations copyright Trish Hill.

British Library Cataloguing in Publication Data.
A Catalogue record for this book is available from the British
Library

ISBN 1 86202 732 3

Designed by designer Pauline McClenahan
Printed in Singapore by PH Productions Pte Ltd

One day, the People Next Door put an enormous sign in front of their house.

The sign said For Sale.

We said, "Thank goodness!"

Sometimes the People Next Door were extremely noisy. They had a barking dog and a loud car, and they often shouted at each other. They got up very early, and they came home late at night. They often honked their car horn and made the engine roar so much that it made our windows rattle.

Sometimes the People Next Door were untidy. They left newspapers on the front steps, and they often forgot to mow their lawn. There were cobwebs in their windows. Their gutters were full of leaves.

The People Next Door could be inquisitive, too. Once, Mrs Next Door leaned over the fence and stared at our vegetable garden. Once, the Kids Next Door climbed a tree and hung there like monkeys snooping at us. Once, Mr Next Door peered into our car and asked where we were going.

So when their For Sale sign went up, we were happy. We looked forward to some quiet, tidy new neighbours. People who knew how to pick up newspapers and how to mind their own business.

People Like Us.

The next Saturday, the People Next Door mowed their lawn. They picked up the newspapers and brushed the cobwebs from their windows.

When we went out onto our porch and had a snack, we saw the People Next Door come out and drive away. Soon after, an estate agent brought clients to look at the house.

Father clicked his tongue. "The husband looks like the type who plays the drums in a rock band," he said. "He probably bangs them all night and that means we'll never get any sleep!"

Mother gasped. "The wife looks like the type who cooks strange food. She'll be boiling weird things all day. We'll never get any fresh air!"

We sniffed. "They look like the type who have no children," we said. "They probably hate kids, and they'll complain about us all the time."

The clients came out of the house next door. They pursed their lips, and they shook their heads. They drove away with the estate agent.

"Thank goodness!" we said.

The estate agent brought another family to look at the house.

Father crossed his legs. "That fellow looks like the type who raises money for charity," he said. "He'll always be knocking at the door, making me give something. We'll go broke."

Mother folded her arms. "That woman looks like the kind who sells cookware to her neighbours. She'll always be stopping me in the street, making me buy something, and we'll end up in the poor house."

We rolled our eyes. "Their children look like the sort who borrow toys and break them. We'll have none left."

After the family looked at the house next door, they shrugged their shoulders and scratched their chins. Then they drove away with the estate agent.

"Phew!" we said.

The next day, the estate agent arrived, followed by an enormous fancy car. We sat up straight and stared. When the people got out of their car, the estate agent hurried to shake their hands. They wore expensive clothes and had fashionable hair styles.

"Now, that's more like it," said Father. "That gentleman looks like he'd give savvy business advice to his neighbours."

"Yes, that's more like it," said Mother. "That lady looks like someone who gives fancy parties and invites her neighbours."

"And those kids look like the type who have great toys to borrow," we said.

After the people looked at the house next door, they wrinkled their noses and brushed their clothes. They pursed their lips and shrugged their shoulders. They looked at our house and scratched their chins. They saw us staring and shook their heads. Then they got into their swanky car and quickly drove away.

"Snobs!" we said. "Thank goodness it won't be them!"

The sun was going down. The People Next Door
came home. They waved to us as their car pulled
up.

"At least the People Next Door are not snobs,"
said Father.

No one seemed to want to buy the house next door. Clients came, shook their heads, and drove away. The For Sale sign began to lean a little. The People Next Door forgot to mow the lawn. New cobwebs appeared on their windows.

"Next Door is becoming a disgrace again," said Mother.

"Just imagine the kind of people who will want to buy it now," said Father. "They will be the kind of people who burn piles of rubbish with clouds of smoke."

"People who leave old cars to rust on their lawn," added Mother. "Or keep dangerous pets, or play loud music."

"Or wear dirty clothes, or shout, or steal," we added.

We looked at one another. "Maybe the People Next Door aren't so bad after all," Mother said.

Father said, "Maybe you're right. Remember the time I was late for work and my car wouldn't start. Mr Next Door saw me and gave me a ride. He was very helpful."

Mother said, "I remember the time all my roses were dying, and I didn't know why. Mrs Next Door saw them and told me how to save them. She was very helpful."

We remembered how frequently the Kids Next Door had let us play in their tree house. The Kids Next Door were okay really, once you got to know them.

Everyone looked at one another, and everyone was thinking the same thing.

We wished the People Next Door wouldn't go. So we came up with a plan to make sure that we would have no new neighbours. We would make sure that the only people living on our street were People Like Us.

For the next two weeks, we didn't mow the grass. We took our curtains down and hung old sheets in our windows. We left newspapers outside so they blew all over the lawn.

When clients came to look at the house next
door, Mother opened our windows and turned up
the radio. She sang songs loudly and off key. She
shouted at us. Father got the car out and worked
on it, banging and clanging and revving the
engine. It made our windows rattle.

We climbed a tree and hung there like
monkeys, scratching our bellies, screeching and
chattering. The clients shook their heads and
drove away.

One morning, the estate agent came and took the For Sale sign away.

"They can't sell their house!" said Father.

"Thank goodness!" we said.

Then the People Next Door came out of their house. We saw them coming up our walk.

"They can't sell their house, and they know it's our fault. They're coming to shout at us!" said Mother.

There was a knock on the door.

Father opened the door a little way and looked out.

Mr and Mrs Next Door stood on the steps. The Kids Next Door were behind them.

"We've just come to thank you," said Mrs Next Door.

"Thank us?" said Father.

"Yes, thank you," said Mr Next Door.

"What for?" asked Mother.

"For helping us," said the Kids Next Door.

Everyone was quiet for a moment.

Finally, Father said, "Come in!"

Everyone sat and stared at one another.
Then Mr Next Door smiled at us.

"We changed our minds about selling our house," said Mr Next Door.

"We wondered what our new neighbours would be like, if we moved," said Mrs Next Door.

"Maybe they would be the kind of people who are snooty," said Mr Next Door.

"Maybe they would be the kind who are snoopy," said Mrs Next Door.

"Or the kind who are selfish," said the Kids Next Door.

"Then we started talking about what nice people you are," said Mr Next Door.

Dad gulped.

"How friendly you always seem," said Mrs Next Door.

Mum blushed.

"How much fun you are to play with," said the Kids Next Door.

We couldn't think of anything to say.

"So, we decided to stay where we had such nice neighbours," said Mr Next Door.

"People who care, and help, and smile," added Mrs Next Door.

"People who share," said the Kids Next Door.

"Our kind of people," they all said.

We knew the kind of people they were talking about.

People Like Us.